FROM
Pain to
Greatness

ANGELLIC CARTER

FROM PAIN TO GREATNESS

By
Angellic C.Carter

ACKNOWLEGMENTS

I would like to first give all the Glory and Honor to my Lord and Savior, for this moment wouldn't be possible without Him. His everlasting mercy and grace which He's shown me during my darkest hours is something I will always forever cherish.

Special thanks to my earthly covering, Pastor Tony Smith of Victorious Ministries International, for his consistent honorable teachings, encouragements, and spiritual guidance through my Wilderness to Victory journey. My mentor, confidant, my sister-in-Christ, and cousin Elder Cheryl Cummings, has been a very influential part in helping me decrease myself so God can increase in me. Elder Cummings never accepted my consistent no-shows to her invitations to visit VMI until I finally showed up; a very powerful woman of God who is always in the business of winning souls for Christ. Minister Rachel Robinson, my God-appointed mentor, ensured that I made it to service each and every week. Very loving, kind, and awesome woman of God who unknowingly gave me so many tools to keep pushing forward towards my salvation, through endless conversation. To my awesome supervisor, sister-in-Christ, and the woman who pushed me into my purpose, Janet Kisyombe, much thanks for consistently expressing to me that someone can benefit from my testimony and the world needs to hear it.

To my loving, caring, and always encouraging daughters, R'Vey Gamble, Destiny Tames, Imani Tames, and Anthonette Carter, I LOVE Y'ALL more than life. Thanks for always believing, supporting, and encouraging me at my lowest points in life. You've changed my life in so many ways and made me see the best in every situation; good, bad, or indifferent, that life has thrown at me. You all are truly God-sent, my earthly angels.

My brothers, Demetreus McGregor, Michael Roseboro, and Marcellus Singletary, will drop anything to come to my rescue at any time. A million Thank you would never be enough. My cousins Toby Roseboro, Kim Hardy, Toni Hardy, Katarsha Hardy, Juanita Sutton, and Neatrice Page who are always on the backline supporting and encouraging me to trust in God through it all.

To my heavenly angels, Alice Singletary-Aiken, if it wasn't for you and your sacrifices there wouldn't be me. Thanks for being the mother you only knew how to be and through your struggles I've learned how to not surrender to my circumstances. You gave me the tools to stand strong against anything that comes at me and taught me to always fight until you can't fight anymore and never give up. Josephine Campbell, my grandmother, was one of the most loving, giving, and loyal individuals who was a prime example of what a strong woman should be. Athena Roseboro, my only sister who no matter what came her way always had utmost faith in God. In every circumstance her reply was, I am waiting on God to heal me, and I know from where I came from. You believed in me when I failed to believe in myself. You took me under your wings as if I was your child and never let me go. You, my sister, became my mother. You fought a long hard fight and never doubted God at all, thatalone was admirable.

PREFACE

Telling my story was me being willing to open up and come to grips with my testimony. This was not an easy process for me and I had to be able to relive my truth to share with others. After much thought and consideration, I felt it was necessary to release my testimony so someone who has found themselves in similar predicaments knows that there's always hope in every encounter they face. First, you must realize that God's timing does not equate to our timing. The God we serve is a Miraculous God and will allow us to be totally broken down so He can build us up in His own image. It takes the willingness of ourselves to step out of the way and allow God to step in and take total control of our brokenness, selfishness, and ourselves. You should never fuss or fight, just have the willingness to stand still and let the transformation take place.

Romans Chapter 12 verse 2- "And do not be conformed to this world, but be transformed by the renewing of your mind, that you may be prove what is that good and acceptable and perfect will of God."

"BE YE TRANSFORMED"

I hope that by allowing you, the reader, to enter into my life you can experience some of my darkest and lowest points in my journeys. That will help you realize that the circumstances and conditions we find ourselves in don't determine our ending. Your continuous belief in God allows you to see peace even in your bad seasons. I can honestly say that during this last year that was designed to utterly destroy me, God gave me so much peace and that's when my faith became even stronger and my Christian journey became much easier. I pray that anyone who is currently facing adversity head on, be willing to let go of their pride and let God do a complete shifting in your life as I had to do. What I also want the reader to take away from this book is that your birth certificate grants you the right to have this earthly and human formation to live your life according to God's will through His words and teachings in the bible.

Deuteronomy Chapter 8 verse 3 - "Man shall not live by bread alone, but man lives by every word that proceeds from the mouth of the LORD."

Table of Contents

CHAPTER ONE
"Lacking Any Type of Faith"

Matthew 6 verse 31- 34 (NKJV)

Therefore, do not worry, saying 'What shall we eat? Or What shall drink? Or What shall we wear? For after all these things the Gentiles seek. For your heavenly Father knows that you need all these things. But seek first the kingdom of God and His righteousness, and all these things shall be added to you. Therefore do not worry about tomorrow, for tomorrow will worry about its own things. Sufficient for the day is its own trouble.

Born on August 30, 1972, into a relationship between my mother and father that was designed to fail from the beginning. Unknowingly, my father was married and his wife, as well as an older brother, resided in another state. Everything my father lacked was being trickled down to me and I was told I lacked as well. When life became difficult for my mother who was now on her own and left to raise four children, it became difficult for me as well. I can't and refuse to speak on what my siblings endured, but I will speak from my perspective. I was the youngest of my siblings and you would honestly think that would make my life easy. I didn't stand a chance, often told that I was not supposed to be here and that I was supposed to

1

have been aborted. That stripped everything from me at a very young age. Self-esteem on zero with a consistent desire to surrender, I was convinced that life would be much easier for me and my parents if I gave up on life.

At 14, I met a young guy who was three years older than me, quiet-natured, and well-spoken that I decided to lose my virginity to. What did I have to lose? If I gave him what he desired then, in turn, he would give me the security and love, that would be more than enough for me. In fact, things were totally opposite. It wasn't enough for either one of us. I wasn't mature enough to handle a senior, and he was too mature to be attached to a freshman. So just as quickly as that relationship began, it ended just the same. My mother had her suspicions that I was sexually active, but instead of dealing with it, I was sent to live down North Carolina with my Dad, a man with whom I only had several brief encounters.

My Dad had no clue on how to raise a teenager nor any interest. The relationship I had with my father was not one of a disciplinarian. It was go to school, work, and take care of yourself. As long as I did that I was more than okay in his eyes. Most children would love that type of carefree relationship, but not me. I just wanted to have a father figure who would stand in correction when I did wrong, sit down and explain to me the birds and the bees, or just say let's go out or something. Since I longed for that from him and he wasn't able to give me those things,

I began to think I wasn't what he wanted or I wasn't good enough to be his daughter. Little did I know my father had many other challenges he was facing and struggling with. Those demons he was chasing had him longing to be in a physical state that wouldn't allow him to be my father or my protector.

I moved into my grandmother's house with a family who knew of me but had no clue who I was in the flesh. In less than six months I was attending computer class and my instructor was informed by my guidance counselor to have me come into her office immediately. I arrived at my guidance counselor's office and was told to close the door behind me and have a seat. Her first question was do I have any family besides my Dad's family. My response was no, not at all. Why do you ask? Because you're no longer able to return to your father's home. Hurt, lost, confused, and tears streaming down my face I couldn't fathom what was happening at that moment. All I knew was I didn't know anyone familiar so now at the age of 16, I was homeless with only my schoolbooks and the clothing on my back. My life felt lifeless, my hope became hopeless, and what little faith I had left was gone. The thought of suicide was becoming more of a reality. I couldn't understand, if there really was a God why would he leave me to fail and suffer in a world so cold? I grew even more confused because I never asked for this life so why was I being betrayed by my family? Especially my Dad. His only job was to protect me and he neglected to do so.

My mother, miles away couldn't help me either, her response was you have to figure it out because I can't get you out of this mess. What mess? I never knew what the reasons were until she informed me that, I brought a man to my grandmother's house and he had been staying there overnight. My voice went from frantic to pure rage and our conversation turned into an argument. I became very disrespectful and never felt apologetic for my actions. How can I have a dude stay at my grandmother's house when my father sleeps by the fireplace in the living room and my grandmother's room was adjacent to the living room? Without notice, I found myself on the phone alone and so upset because I never even had a chance to voice my opinion on the situation.

My integrity was in question and no one cared to hear nor ask if was there any truth to this lie. All I knew was I had to find somewhere to go and I had until the close of the school day to accomplish that. My mother called to the school a few hours later and informed my guidance counselor that she found me somewhere to reside at my Aunt's house, but she was not sending me to come back to Baltimore. I never met my aunt until I moved in with her, she was a very pleasant, honorable, and respectable woman who was raising her two granddaughters. I resided with them until I graduated from high school.

My plans were to go into the United States Coast Guard, but that was an epic fail, so I opted to go to the Atlanta Job Corps.

I arrived in Atlanta via Greyhound bus, the first few weeks I was distant and trying to make the best out of a situation until I did better. It wasn't long before I began interacting and becoming more social with the other girls there. I became best friends with Michele and Melissa, we were considered a ruthless bunch. You wouldn't see one without the other. We stayed in the midst of everything that happened, if one fight we all fought, and eventually that landed us in jail numerous times. On one occasion, we were breaking up a fight and because of our reputations, we were arrested for being guilty by association. My outlet for stress relief was marijuana and alcohol. I was either on restriction for sneaking out after curfew or my attitude. I was 17 years old, 5'11, and size 0 so there was nothing anyone could say to me. I began smelling myself.

I met this student named Raymond and we hit it off from our first encounter in class. I would sneak over to his mother's house frequently and it got to the point she liked me so much on my weekend passes I would stay with him without any issues. We dated for over two years until I got kicked out of Atlanta Job Corps and sent back on the first plane back to Baltimore for fighting and punching a hole in the cafeteria wall. That was the breaking point for the director of the facility and I couldn't blame him. He gave me so many breaks due to my family situation, and even sent me to counseling as well as Alcoholics Anonymous just to keep me off the streets. As much as he wanted to save me this last time, he couldn't because his supervisor was totally against it due to the reputation attached to my name. What I failed to realize is that every action has a reaction. I knew it was a matter of time before I was going to get expelled. I was told that I had to choose whether to return to Shelby, North Carolina, or head back to Baltimore, Maryland. For me neither choice was a good one, I didn't want to stay with my mother or father, but my mother was the better of the two. Baltimore was familiar and more suitable to my environment, so that's what I chose.

I arrived back in Baltimore via Delta Airlines and was so disappointed in myself for again putting myself into this situation, not only was I going to hear my mother's mouth about my failures she was going to let everyone else know as well. My brother picked me up at the airport with his wife and children. They took me to get something to eat and then I arrived at my mother's residence. The welcoming was much better than I imagined, but that situation was short-lived. I was told I needed to find a job as soon as possible and take care of myself. So I did that with the help of my mother, she was friends with the owners of Bill's Carryout and I was offered a job and maintained that job for 12 years alongside employment at the University of Maryland Medical Center.

One day after working 17 hours at Bill's, I returned to my mother's residence and I couldn't get in and she wouldn't answer the door. So at 4 am, I was locked out scrambling to find where I would go. My boss waited to assure me I would get in but to no avail. I called my sister and she invited me to reside with her until I was able to obtain housing. I heard from my mother days later, and she told me that I couldn't come to her house because her boyfriend had returned home and didn't want me to be there. It hurt like hell because once again I needed my mother and she failed me. At that moment my attitude shifted and my heart became cold. I found myself becoming distant with everyone. I was at work one evening and my emotions began to get the best of me.

My suicidal thoughts were now my reality and I took a whole bottle of pain pills and began feeling dizzy and faint. I was rushed to the hospital and was kept for observation. The only person who visited was my boyfriend, who did not leave my side not even for a minute. After being discharged I felt ashamed and it appeared that I was at the lowest point of my life. I had no desire to live. I was living but wasn't existing, just accepting the minimum out of life. I went to see a therapist at work and her solution I felt was medication to help with my anxieties and depression. After a week on the medication, I made the decision to stop taking it and try to figure things out on my own.

At 22, I met a guy at work and later we had two daughters together, Imani and Destiny. Together we realized that we were unequally yoked and ended the relationship. We've remained close for the sake of our children which was a long process. Yes, we had our ups and downs like everyone else, but for the first time in my life, I had a positive outcome in a relationship. I refuse to speak of the details of this relationship, because no matter what occurred the good always outweighed the bad. We became more like family and the boundaries were never crossed. Our focus was geared more towards raising our girls in a positive environment.

I received an unexpected call from my cousin stating that she had someone looking for me and wanted to talk to me -- a blast from the past. He was locked down in federal prison for over 15 years. When he got on the phone it took me by total surprise. As far as I was concerned I was completely done with that relationship years ago. The conversation went very well, he asked to stop by and see me face-to-face. Not even an hour later who was at my apartment door, Mr. Collins, the blast from my past. Still in the custody of the federal prison system in a halfway house, we decided to take things slow and see what would come of the relationship. Things progressed very quickly and every Friday he was released for the weekend to either his mother's house or mine on a pass, but had to be in either residence in time to do a phone check-in. I still maintained my employment at the University of Maryland Medical Systems in the Pulmonary Functions Laboratory, as an administrative assistant making great wages.

Still in custody, he was employed with a moving company making good money but it wasn't enough to maintain the previous lifestyle that he was accustomed to. When we grew up he was known for being a drug kingpin and that was the life he was trying to recapture. I would be lying if I said I was opposed to it because I wasn't at all. Never quit my job and he never asked me to either, but all my bills were paid by him and money was available at my disposal. Never once did he ask what I needed money for, I just got it and spent it for me and my children. My children were like his, he never discredited anything their father did, he loved them and they lacked for nothing. Shopping and spending time with my girls and his son was how we passed the time on numerous occasions. He would do random pop-ups on my job with lunch when he thought our relationship was going to end or we had a blown-out argument. Holidays were always great times with his family. There was nothing my girls as well as his son asked for they didn't receive, if I said no he would go behind my back and purchased it.

Months later I found out I was pregnant and six months into the pregnancy lost our child. That's when things started going downhill, I was the blame for the miscarriage because I wouldn't take care of myself, let him tell it. As much as he proclaimed to be okay, truthfully speaking, he really wasn't. Honestly, my love never changed for him, but we lived in the same house and rarely saw each other except when we came home together at the end of the evening. I knew that things were coming to a breaking point either we were going to work on our relationship issues or let it go. He wanted us to try again at having another child and I wasn't against to the idea. I became pregnant and things began to turn around for us, we began reconnecting and rebuilding.

Several months later he picked me up from work and had business to take care of, so I was dropped off at my cousin's house for a few hours, then we were to go out to dinner and see a movie. When conducting his business dealings he made sure that I was nowhere in sight of it. I became very upset because I called his phone when it was getting late. He was finishing up business and stated he would see me soon. I was getting worried when he didn't answer the next time I called and didn't receive and answer because we heard gunshots. We didn't know where they were coming from, so I asked my cousin to just take me home, because I was tired of waiting. As we were leaving her they were coming from

and she proceeded to take me home. For some reason, my nervousness grew because anytime I called he answered and this was way out of character for him. I arrived at my house and realized my house key was on the same key chain as his car keys, so my cousin and I climbed up the fire escape.

As I approached the window my house phone was ringing. I finally got inside and missed the call. Then it rang again and on the other end was his mother telling me he had been shot and rushed to Shock Trauma, it wasn't looking good. By the time I arrived at the hospital, his mother started walking towards me accompanied by her brother with tears in both of their eyes. His mother said I needed to come with her, we walked down the hallway, and when we got on the elevator that's when I received the news that he didn't make it. We were escorted to the trauma room where his lifeless body was laying partially covered by a white sheet and all I could think was how did this happen? We had plans and I was pregnant with his child. The nurse said that he was a very pleasant man and her heart goes out to us because he fought until he couldn't fight anymore. The close impact of the bullets ripped his insides apart and there wasn't anything for the surgeons to connect.

After the funeral I grew more depressed, I decided

that I wasn't raising a child without their father and I had an abortion. I decided it was time for me to relocate from

our apartment for my safety as well as my two daughters. We took residence on Pennsylvania Avenue and after a year or more decided it was time for me to move on with my life, not date but just get my life in order. I had my apartment for at least six months and never stayed in it. After some time, I decided that since I was going to live there and make the best out of it. I finally brought new furniture and fixed the place up. I had to get myself together for my girls and find some stability in our lives after this tragedy. I maintained steady employment and my girls were well taken care of. I stayed to myself because didn't want any issues from any of the other residents in that complex.

Several months later I met one of the residents and we became very good friends. We watched out for each other as well as our children. Two residents became very jealous of our bond and their main objective was to cause conflict between both of us and were very successful at it. That made me very secluded. One day coming home from work, I found the maintenance man sitting on the steps by my apartment, very attractive, tall, slim, with braided hair, which was the ultimate turn-on for me, very soft-spoken, and as I was approaching my door, he said that he been working in my apartment all day doing repair orders and was about to finish up. A few minutes later he entered my unit after me and was working in my kitchen. He asked if was I currently seeing anyone, at that particular time I was dating but not attached. We exchanged numbers and from that day forward we spoke on the phone from time to time, then after a month's time we connected on another level, sexually.

I was very stubborn and many times when it came to dating I believed that if a man doesn't call you then you shouldn't stress yourself out by continuously chasing after him. One of two things was happening, he wasn't impressed with your encounter, or he wanted you to chase after him. I wasn't the type to do either. After our third sexual encounter, I became pregnant by a man who said he was unable to have children and that's when his denial began. I called him from work to let him know that I was pregnant and he straight denied my child. He avoided me until my baby girl was 2 months old and he decided that we needed to talk after I got fed up with the rumors that were circulating around my apartment complex. The rumors are not what bothered me, because my late grandmother always stated that the truth deserves no explanation.

As hurt as I was about his actions, it began to take a toll on me, not only was I dealing with my issues with him, but the death of my sister who passed away right before my eyes. Athena was my only sister as well as my best friend, confidant, and the only individual who could keep me sane, literally. I dropped from a size 12 to a size

8, due to depression and was unable to function or fully present in my own life. My girls were never neglected and we had a bond that was inseparable. They loved on my baby girl like no other and my neighbor, Sheri and I reconnected again and she always came and got my baby girl as well as my older two girls just so I could get a break. He came to talk but little did he know I didn't want to hear anything that wasn't about my child's birth certificate and his signature. He signed her birth certificate without hesitation, but his conversation wasn't about being a part of my child's life, it was more geared to wanting to reconnect sexually. I didn't want to hear any of it, my conversations were about the hurt and humiliation he caused in my life because I knew an apology was not going to happen. Truth be told, his arrogance and pride wouldn't allow him to give it to me.I was very bitter towards him especially since he knew about all the complications and hospitalizations I had experienced during my pregnancy.

Months later I got fed up with his continuous no-shows to see our child. I was told by a resident that he was denying my child, so I went up to his apartment and gained entry, went straight to his door, and proceeded to bang on it until he answered the door. When he finally answered we got into a shouting match and every feeling and emotion that I had for the past year was unleashed. Then at that very moment, all he could do was stare in disbelief as I uttered the words from my mouth and turned to exit his building. Moments later he arrived at my building and went off on my neighbor as I kicked his car door. The older two children's father was shocked as well because of the whole incident and as I stated previously we had become very good friends as well as family. He was there because our daughters were in the marching band and had a parade that day. As he pulled off, my phone began to ring and he was on the other end asking can we talk. I went into a neighbor's apartment and we spoke for almost an hour.

Apologetically, he stated that he wanted us to work on being able to communicate so we could co-parent together, and then work on being together to raise our child. I never took him seriously because of all the womanizing he had done in the past with residents, so I said whatever. My instincts were right all along, his cellphone records confirmed it. I switched his line to mine after I found several numbers on my bill. One number called and when I answered she stated the wrong number, then proceeded to call back. This time she had questions for me and I let her ask all she needed to. Then I had questions and I explained to her that I didn't have an issue with her because she had done nothing wrong to me. So we decided to meet up at his apartment. I found out that while I helped him get a car to keep from losing his job, she signed the title because he couldn't get insurance in his name unbeknownst to me. So he thought he was just meeting me at his apartment and when I arrived at his house I was alone but she had her mother and family with her.

The mother approached me with good intentions to resolve the matter and when he arrived of course he tried to turn the tables as if he didn't want anything to do with her. I couldn't do anything with the car because it wasn't registered to me so I took the loss of $800, grabbed the keys from his hands, and gave them to her. We didn't speak for over a week after this incident, he couldn't say anything that could impress me because in my mind I was done. My heart said otherwise, but my mind was made up at this point. As far as I was concerned my hopes for trusting another man were out of the question. That was November, then December came around and he started to visit with our daughter. We became more connected because his feelings were present and visible through his actions. I received the key to his apartment and on that same day Christmas Eve, he proposed to me with a beautiful ring. We decided to get married months later on his birthday June 21, 2007, at the courthouse and have our reception and reading of our vows in a different ceremony. I honestly thought that my marriage would be my escape from self-imprisonment, but that was far from the case.

What were my personal feelings about my father and mother growing up? If they were alive today and I was allowed to speak my truth what would I have the courage to say?

Dear Parents of Mine,

Throughout the years I had so much animosity, frustration, and hate toward both of you. I always felt that the two of you were some selfish ass people. Why? Because if you knew that in your hearts you couldn't see fit to love me and nurture me like a newborn, toddler, and teenager deserved to be, why create me? I needed y'all throughout the years and I often felt that if y'all knew then that you wouldn't love me, why not use protection? Better than that, why not just go ahead with the abortion process or not lay the fuck down at all! You'll never know how it felt to be mentally confined to the 4 x 4 prison cell I was trapped in because of y'all. Why produce a life to mentally, physically, and emotionally abuse me? Y'all don't need to answer, because at that place I was in I don't need a lame-ass excuse from either one of y'all. I was innocent, I was your child, and I had so many beautiful gifts locked down inside of me that I was unable to properly develop. I didn't have a chance how to unlock them and share them with the world. Y'all stole that from me. This wasn't about either one of y'all at all. I didn't ask for this life, it was chosen for me. It hurt like hell that I was trapped in this mental state of being so fucked up that I couldn't decipher what tools I needed to use to survive. I couldn't even tell what it actually felt like to be loved or even know how to properly love my damn self. What y'all did to me throughout the years was so heartbreaking. Y'all gave me to the world without warning or notice, as if y'all didn't give a damn how your own flesh and blood would survive. Then y'all of all people judged me and became two of my worst critics. Did you ever stop, think, or even care about the impact that those behaviors would have on me now? Often lost and mentally fucking confused. Have y'all thought that I owe it to this child to become better, and get the necessary help to overcome whatever it was that had you distracted? I seriously doubt you ever did. It hurts me like hell to reminisce about my past. Many times I would mentally say, "I WISH I WAS DEAD", but at a point it was my reality, not to help you feel at ease, but to escape from the mental hell I had succumbed to. Do you know at times I honestly felt guilty for even waking up? Because truth be told my life could've been given to someone more deserving and worthy of living it. Y'all created an ugly and worthless child. Someone who struggled because she didn't have the willpower or tools to uncover her own riches and glory. I was y'all escape, punching bag, doormat, and everything you'll hate about each other. Y'all abandoned me straight from the womb. Now y'all both exited this world and left me behind to deal with the dysfunction I inherited from both of y'all. Now mentally my struggles have tripled, yes we're all now together finally. Your trust issues and low self-esteem, I inherited that as well. Mission accomplished, job well done. Are you satisfied now?

The day of my birth, August 30, 1972, was the day that y'all signed over y'all God-given rights. Every photo I have comes from a relative. I often asked myself over the years, because I could never recall, did I ever get a hug (that warm motherly or fatherly embrace), I LOVE YOU, kiss, or JOB WELL DONE. It was as if y'all never felt the need to invest in me at all. If you say otherwise, I never heard it. So over the years, I learned to accept those things, I never expected to ever hear those words uttered from the mouths of my very own birth parents. I wish y'all could've walked a mile in my shoes, but that would make me heartless and cold. Why? Because I would never want anyone to endure that type of pain. The consistent inappropriate touching at the hands of a grown coward ass man, (my stepfather) the mental anguish, the self-inflicted wounds, and the image of me standing in a mirror not recognizing the reflection staring back at me. It was as if I was an empty lifeless vessel of a human being. That invasion of an innocent child is a subject that I was forced to keep hidden for years because it was the fear of what my brothers and family would do to his trifling ass as well as the embarrassment.

My voice was silenced at the age of 7 by my

mother when she ended her relationship with that

piece of trash sick bastard. You told him to get his shit and get out, but that wasn't what did it for me. At that very moment I thought I found refuge for once, but what followed next put me back in mental turmoil. Laying on my bed hearing you utter out of your mouth for him to "take her fast ass with you" when he left. What made you seriously think that he had any capability of raising me when he was consistently physically abusing you? In his fucked-up eyes this 7-year-old looked like a grown-ass woman and you knew that. I was your child and your baby girl. Your breaking point for him should've been on Bruce Street, truth be told when you caught him peeking through the bathroom door when I was bathing, or when I was in the basement eating breakfast and you noticed me crying as he was stroking my hair. I told you he was making me uncomfortable at that time and you told me to shut the hell up and I better stop lying like that. My sister Athena was my confidant and we shared rooms so she did her best to protect me as much as she could. He had you so damn convinced that she was a damn problem child because she probably was the first one to ever stand up to his punk ass. So on his word, you sent away the only person at that time who protected me away to Villa Maria, a place for troubled youth. As my mother realizing that her behavior was because she did what you failed as a damn mother to do, protected her sister and your child. This is the same no-good bastard you forced me to call Daddy. I really needed you MOTHER, and you left me. I still have nightmares about him and the smell of his stinking ass body scent. Why didn't you send me down North Carolina then, instead of waiting till I got older and started dealing with a drug dealer?

DAD, oh please don't think you're exempt from this shit at all. Had you stood up and accepted your responsibilities as a man this wouldn't have ever happened. I never saw or heard from you when you left to go to North Carolina. I didn't see or hear from you until years later when you moved back to rekindle things with my mother, but that was short-lived. Who protected your child when someone attempted steal their innocence? No one did. What state did you leave me in, when y'all silenced my voice and ignored my cries? Y'all left me vulnerable, confused, and looking for the love I desired from the two of you in the worst place, in the arms of teenage boys and grown men that saw a well-shaped girl, long hair, and damaged soul that they only wanted to feel the warmth of her vagina. They couldn't see past that to unlock my value, because I couldn't see past it either. We never had the talk that a Father and Daughter are supposed to have. I thought that through my cloudiness, if we were connected sexually they would stay around. As a FATHER you never gave me the courage to not settle or save myself for the right time and someone much deserving of it. I've seen fathers interact with their daughters over the years and I never received that from you, so I envied and longed for that.

I will conclude now because the more I reflect on my past the angrier I get. I'm trying to see past this prison cell y'all put me in and sentence me to death by mental suicide. I hope y'all understand that I had to get these things off my chest, so I can try to enjoy the next stage of my life. If you can't understand my frustration let's just say I don't care, because for the life of me, I could never understand the actions of y'all as either.

Sincerely,

Your lost, confused, and heartbroken daughter

CHAPTER TWO
"I Just Didn't Fit In"

Isaiah chapter 43 verses 1 – 3

"Fear not, for I have redeemed you; I have called you by your name, you are Mine. When you pass through the waters, I will be with you, and through the rivers, they shall not overflow you. When you walk through the fire, you shall not be burned, nor shall the flame scorch you. For I am the LORD your God, the Holy One of Israel, your Savior"

Have you ever felt as if you come up short or don't fit in when you're in the company of certain family, friends, and associates? For me that's always been the case, I'm present physically, but mentally it's a totally different story. I can't quite describe it, but things they felt comfortable doing, weren't so comfortable to me. I also felt different. As if I didn't belong in their presence or just didn't quite live up to their standards. For instance, in my marriage, I was excited to get married, but as I reflect on the events leading up to it, I can honestly say what should have been a happy time frame for me it really wasn't. I loved the man I was to marry, but was I in love with the fact that I was getting a man whom others desired or just the thought of not being alone? I prayed to God over the course of my pregnancy that He make my situation better so that I could bring my child up in a family setting. I asked God to make this man my husband, to have and to hold, for richer and poorer, till death do us part. What I lacked to ask God was to make him in His image. My life was not godly, so I gave satan full authority over me.

Things I accepted throughout my marriage were wrong but I wasn't willing to say I failed, so I did what was necessary to keep my life intact in the public eye. Knowing full well that privately I was living in a self-made prison. Two years into my marriage my father-in-law passed. The day before the funeral I found out my husband had four other daughters by four different women by a sister who couldn't wait to disclose it. Instead of addressing the situation, I covered it up with a quick comeback at her and made my exit from his mother's home. I was told by him, as well as his mother, that she was lying and on the drive back home all I wanted to do was pack my things up and return to my apartment. I loved his family as my own so I took his word, as well as his mother's, and let the situation go. The next day we arrived at his mother's house to follow in the funeral procession and as we were riding this weird, unexplainable feeling came over me. When we lined up with the family he was a little distant from me as if we were just friends, and he was just conversing with my stepfather who came to support him.

As we sat down I took notice of this little girl sitting in front of us, she looked just like my daughter, just darker in complexion and she waved at him, then said hello. He was hesitant to respond until I asked who she was, his response took me by complete surprise. "That's my daughter." In complete and utter shock out of respect for my surroundings, I couldn't even respond, but at that point, my heart broke. After the funeral we had two other encounters with two of his other children, one was pregnant and he introduced us, the other he denied. Emotions at an all-time high, I decided that it was best for me to ride with his nephew and niece to the cemetery to avoid any other lies.

I have always been told whether they're family or not you stand behind the truth, if they're wrong let them know they are wrong. For me, I take family and friendships very personally, so to be consistently around my in-laws and everyone know the truth except me, I felt betrayed. I would be lying to myself if I said I forgave them because that's far from the truth. On holidays I would come around, but instead of pitching in and helping out like I used to, I would sit in the living room and watch everyone else enjoy themselves. On Thanksgiving, I opted to stay home because as much as I tried to fit in, I honestly didn't. I decided to surround myself with my children, their friends, and my older two daughters' father, his wife, her brother, and his father whom I called Dad. A lot of people think that when a relationship is over tension and animosity should take place. But being mature enough to say this relationship is not the best thing for us and create bonds and ties like family. That's the type of relationship my older children's father and I have. His wife is like a sister and we all go out and have great times together without confusion. I made a vow to myself to not try to fit into situations that were not conducive to my life. If it takes me out of my comfort zone then it's not where I need to be.

Luke Chapter 8 verse 17

For nothing is secret that will not be revealed, nor anything hidden that will not be known come to light.

For many years I tried to mimic the life my late grandmother lived, taking care of everyone, but lacking in taking care of myself. As long as my husband, children, and family were okay then I would be okay. That was far from the reality of things. I knew something in my life had to change and if it didn't I was destined to have another nervous breakdown, or stroke due to unnecessary stress. I put on so many unwanted pounds and went from a size 12 to a size 22 in a matter of four years. The mirror was my worst enemy. I wasn't happy about what it reflected, the hurt, self-neglect, and image of what I had succumbed to. I decided to do a transformation in my life and drop the unwanted pounds.

I was very successful at my weight loss journey, and the weight was gone, but unfortunately, the problems weren't. One day I requested to leave early because I wasn't feeling well and my nurse manager had no problem granting me that request. She stated that if I said I wasn't feeling well then it must be true because of my work ethic. I never called out on my days off. I was working, to be exact, every week I was clearing anywhere from 60-70 hours a week. Not because I wanted to but because I was the sole provider in my family and if bills weren't met it was on me. I arrived home and went to my room by passing my husband who was sitting in the living room playing video games and went straight to my room and passed out in a matter of minutes. I awakened hours later feeling weak and dizzy, went to the bathroom, showered, and washed my face all in hopes of shaking those feelings, but to no avail. I went to reach for my toothbrush and my legs completely gave out on me. I called for help but no one heard me so I sat on the floor for a few minutes trying to catch my breath and gain some strength to get up. I managed to make my way to my bed and rest my back against the side because of its high platform. I was able to retrieve my cellphone and I called my husband's phone. He answered and responded, give him a few minutes, he wanted to finish up what he was doing which was playing his video game. I called my daughter who resided in the basement but she was asleep and didn't answer.

I had to get to the emergency room, so I put my shoes on and made my way to the car, and drove myself, not uttering one word to my husband as he sat on the couch. I arrived at Good Samaritan Hospital emergency department, parked my car, and checked myself in. Moments later at triage, I was immediately taken to the back and helped into a bed, and started on fluids because my blood pressure was below normal limits and my heart rate was elevated. The nurse gave me medication to help with the nausea and vomiting that I began experiencing, then I went to sleep. I don't know how long I was asleep but I was awakened by the attending physician asking me what happened and how did I get to this point. The attending ordered a full panel of blood work and a CAT scan to see if I had any other issues going on. I waited for some time for all my results to come and quickly fellback to sleep, only to be awakened several hours later by the charge nurse. The charge nurse stated that due to my laboratory work which showed below-normal blood pressure, and an elevated heart rate they wanted to admit me to the hospital. I signed all the paperwork and called to let my husband know what was going on and his response was heartbreaking. He didn't know who was going to watch my daughter, our child, because he had dialysis and other things he had to do. I hung up the phone and began crying because no matter what issues or hospitalizations he faced I was right by his side and the moment I really needed him I couldn't get his support. My daughter called my cellphone and asked where I was, my husband never told her that I went to the emergency room. I told her not to worry, I signed myself out, waited to get my prescriptions then I went home.

I arrived home, went to my room and who followed me, my husband trying to apologize, but that fell straight on deaf ears. At that point I just needed him to go back to his couch and leave me the hell alone. Nothing he could say or do would make me feel good about him or my marriage. For several days I laid in my bed and with the help of my oldest daughter, who filled the gap for my baby girl, so I could rest. Little did I know that during this week I would receive a Facebook invitation from my cousin Cheryl. The message was that she would like for all her family to come to church with her on that Sunday. I decided that she was being persistent for a reason. Before then, Cheryl invited me to church for an event she was having. I went as far as purchasing the ticket but never showed up. I felt as if it was time to show up and support her.

That Sunday, I got up out the bed, got dressed, and made my way into Victorious Ministries International, expecting nothing at all but to say I finally came to support her. I've always been the type to observe my surroundings before engaging in any type of activities, I didn't care what the circumstances were. I arrived in my normal fashion, late, so I missed the first song during praise and worship. By the time I was allowed to enter, I spotted my cousins and joined them. I got so emotional during Praise and Worship because the music was ministering to me, but I fought back the tears. Then when Pastor Smith came out and delivered his sermon, I was totally at a loss for words. I don't remember the topic at all, but what I do recall is that he was speaking about my situation. I listened to every word that came forth from his mouth and when he did the altar call, I came with the expectation of just receiving a prayer. What I left with was a prayer and conviction. After service ended, I quickly gave my cousins hugs and exited as soon as I could to keep from breaking down emotionally in front of anyone. I got in my car, started it up and literally sat in it for 30 minutes crying and called my cousin Imelda to explain what just happened. I ended the conversation with her still in tears as I drove home in complete silence -- no radio. I had one brief encounter listening to Pastor Smith speak and that was at my aunt's funeral.

I pulled in front of my house and sat there for a moment once I saw my husband's car was still parked in the same spot since I left. I had to contemplate what I would encounter as I walked through the door. For the first time in years, I actually prayed on something. I entered my house and checked on my baby girl who was in her room awaiting my return. She gathered her stuff and climbed in my bed and we conversed for a little before we both took a nap. I received a call from my cousin Cheryl asking did I enjoyed service and I actually told her I would definitely be back that following Sunday with my baby girl.

That next Sunday I got up early and prepared baby girl's clothing as well as mine for church. We showered and got dressed, then made our way to Victorious Ministries for 11 am service. We were asked by one of the greeters to sit on the second row. Praise and worship was again ministering to my situation, emotions on high, and eyes watery from trying to fight back my tears. Pastor Tony Smith gave an excellent sermon and somewhere in the course of it, he told me to go home, pack my bags, and prepare to move. In awe, I was like who is this man talking to? He has no clue what I'm going through, how dare he make that call I've been here twice. This man needs to mind his business, so it's safe to say I didn't take it seriously at all. I admire his teaching methods and his realness so I would definitely be back. I might consider this my church home, so I needed to be patient and not move too swiftly and get disappointed.

From October to December, I felt more convicted by every service I attended. The one sermon that the Pastor brought forth really grabbed my attention was ''Rebuilding.'' It was much needed. He spoke on having a plan, passion, staying focused, visions, and distractions. People tend to think that most of the time when I'm quiet that either I'm that person by nature or that something is bothering me. That's far from the case. When I'm quiet my mind is constantly meditating on things I've learned or heard that gained my interest, whether current or past.

With that being said, I couldn't understand for the life of me why I never fit into my surroundings easily. Then reflecting on the knowledge I've obtained through church as well as my cousin Cheryl. I realized it was God setting me apart so he could change my character and I could surrender myself to live according to His will and serve Him. I've lost some relationships with family and friends throughout my prison to victory journey. It bothered me but I came to the realization that everyone can't hop aboard the bus on your journey to where God is leading you. When God is setting you apart it's not to make you look down on people at all and people fail to realize that. When going through the process of growth in the will of God, old habits must die and mindsets have to shift, or you're just a living empty vessel. My drinking, wicked tongue, reckless attitude, and many other bad habits that altered my thinking had to die. It was time that I set those bad habits on fire and walked away and did not try to extinguish the flames or relationships that I left behind.

I just didn't fit in because the plans God had for my life were something I didn't have a clear view of until I started getting convicted. Being willing to be set apart for God meant I had to learn to step out on faith and trust in our Father wholeheartedly while casting all doubts aside. The most challenging part was surrendering when the stubborn and self-righteous me thought I could solve everything on my own. We as individuals must be fully aware that God's positioning of us was designed so we could complete the vision He set forth for us. We must also understand why God set us apart and stop trying to predict the outcome. For only our God knows our outcome. You can't let others determine your outcome. In the process of being set apart, you will be hurt by people, but everything you do must be connected to God. Trust me, the price and sacrifices of losing old habits and people are worth the blessing. You have to protect everything God is connecting you to, and if you don't have the shield of faith (The Bible), you will remain in your self-made prison longer than you have to. Release your hands off of what God has freed you from. That season has passed, and you're no longer there. He is elevating you to the next level and freeing you from the old you. Time to let go of the bondage and release those self-made shackles.

Proverbs Chapter 14 verse 12 -

"There is a way that seems right to a man,
But its end is the way of death."

CHAPTER THREE
"I Am Justified"

Romans Chapter 3:24

Being justified freely by His grace through the redemption that is in Christ Jesus

Galatians Chapter 2:16

knowing that a man is not justified by the works of the law but by faith in Jesus Christ, even if we have believed in Christ Jesus, that we might be justified by faith in Christ and not by the works of the law' for by the works of the law no flesh shall be justified

There's a lane somewhere and it has my name on it. I can honestly say that after suffering so many temporary attacks in my life, there has to be a reward coming along for me. I just have to stick to the script and let God continue to order my footsteps. I have to let my faith put a down payment on my destiny and I have to allow God to transition me into a new me. I'm so committed to my future and I refuse to look back. I placed post-it notes on my bedroom mirror as daily reminders to keep me encouraged, not go astray, and always reflect on these things. It was a brilliant idea I came up with, but as I began to walk in a way that was pleasing to

God, the devil kept releasing attacks from theconfines of my own house.

You may think that my grammar is off because throughout this book I've been using the terminology "house" instead of "home" but let me give you a brief overview of that. I take pride in decorating, painting, and designing each home I lived in, they were my sanctuary, an escape from the world. When I enter my home I want it to make me feel comfortable in all aspects, décor means everything to me. That's my comfort zone as well as shopping. A paintbrush and paint can turn the most unflattering places into a palace. That's the type of environment I love to create for me and my girls.

As I transitioned from my apartment into my husband's residence, I had to loosen up a little. I never put a television in my living room because that was my showroom, now I had to change that concept. I was willing to give in for the sake of creating an environment that was comfortable for my entire family. For several years throughout my marriage, I periodically changed my mental décor according to the situation I was in. The last house we resided in as a married couple, I was there for a year and never put my bedroom together, let alone my house. It was a beautiful structure and newly renovated, but I never once took pride in it, I will go as far as saying I didn't care about it because my marriage was a total mess and my children were beginning to act hostile like the environment we created.

On my days off from work, after I dropped my baby girl off to school, I wouldn't return home. I treated myself to breakfast, spent time at the mall shopping for myself and my baby girl, paid bills, and did Bodywerk just to stay away from my house and husband. That house never felt like a home for me, not one bit. When I was in that house the arguments got so intense I would start hitting so deep with words below the belt. I would let him say what he wanted then when he was finished I would unleash my sharp tongue and wouldn't stop until I made him feel like he made me feel for years. My tongue was my defense in so many arguments not only with my husband but with anyone that came at me wrong. I didn't take pride in that side of me because it was a very dark and angry place that I hated going to. I will admit that I did feel justified for my tongue even though I know for sure some things I should've just walked away.

As my faith grew I knew that I had to step back and let God fight the battles, but I was still living in another man's time. Still stuck in a place that God was trying to release me from. Every argument was leading me right back to the place I kept consistently praying to God to remove me from. I kept letting my pride and attitude set me back from my breakthrough. I was on the run and I was becoming more hopeless as far as my marriage was concerned. That whole situation wasn't working in my favor, it was lowering me day by day.

One Sunday in February, baby girl and I arrived at church and she gave me a hug and out of the blue said, "Mommy no matter what I will always love you and I won't be upset if Daddy leaves." At a loss for words, I hugged her so tight and said Thank you. I needed to hear that. The Altar call came and Pastor Tony walked down from the Pulpit and came towards where we were standing, grabbed my hands, and whispered into my ear, "Don't be afraid to move, if you don't move God will destroy everything you won't let go." I broke down in tears and began praying to God like never before to help me move and give me the strength to walk away in complete peace while renewing my mind. It's time and I'm in need of you Lord. I don't want to play it safe anymore, I need You to stretch me and whatever purpose You have for my life, use me. I'm tired of the prison, I'm tired of the self-inflected wounds, I'm tired of giving of myself and making investments with no return, I'm tired of being sick and tired, I'm tired of looking whole on the outside and being a filthy mess on the inside, I NEED YOU LORD AND I NEED YOU NOW. Doing things on my own is not working, taking care of everybody and everything is slowly killing me and I don't know how much longer I can live like this. I need You to touch me and revive everything in me that's dead. I'm tired of arriving D.O.A. (Dead on Arrival) in every situation pertaining to my life.

My prayer life needed to increase in my death season and I had to learn to call out to the Lord at this time. "God save me, deliver me, shift my atmosphere, and do a rapid shifting for my girls as well. Rain down your Holy Spirit into me and fill all my emptiness like only You know how. In the name of the Almighty Jesus Christ." Then things started moving swiftly, my husband got fed up with our marriage and went to the emergency room with complaints of abdominal pains. My opinion is that he knowingly did this since as a Dialysis patient he knew it would result in him being admitted for observation overnight. Once I found out from Facebook that he was being admitted I called him and said I was coming as soon as I left work. His response was, "I'm good, my brother will be here with me, and don't act as if you're concerned". All I could respond was okay, there was nothing else to be said. The next day I was off work, I dropped my baby girl off at school and went back home to take a quick nap before I met my cousin for brunch. My phone rang and all I heard was "you act as if you don't care, and you could've at least come to check on my brother. I thought you were a much better person than this, guess I was wrong, and after all my family has done for you and your children."

"You finished?", was my response, but he kept running his mouth so I had to shut it down, but this time I was going to do it differently than expected. "First of all, please tell me what you and your family have done for me and my kids, and let me make it clear, my kids don't lack for a damn thing, especially my older girls. I never asked anyone in your family to EVER pay one bill, buy me food, get me a job, or anything, so have a nice day". As he was speaking I hit the end button with the quickness. Yes, I was mad, but truth be told how can I get mad over lies, especially when the person feeding the foolishness was a master manipulator, Narcissist, as well as a chronic liar? I can say that because I witnessed it first-hand. I could've easily turned the tables and stated things I've done, but like I said before, the truth needs no explanation. They can have that, I'm officially done, but let's be really clear, I personally feel that if an allegedly grown man gets another man to call and check his wife it's time to keep moving forward.

I tell you with everything in me that I truly thank God for that shifting because, at this point, He put my tongue on life support. The phone rang again and who was on the other end, my husband. I let it continue to ring because there was nothing and I repeat nothing he could've said that I wanted to hear. Then I received a text saying that he was going to stay at his brother's house until I learned to respect him. Okay cool, if that's what you want to do then so be it, have a nice life, was my response. That was the break I really needed and didn't realize it until I was able to sleep a whole night without wondering when the next argument was going to occur or having to listen to him talk recklessly about me on the phone in code, like I was so naïve to understand. My marriage hurt me so bad that I made a vow to myself that very day that I was going to refuse to open up or put faith again in another man unless God was in him and He let me know it was time.

Psalms Chapter 147 verses 3 through 7

3 He heals the brokenhearted and binds up their wound, 4 He counts the number of the stars; he calls them all by name. 5 Great is our Lord, and mighty in power; His understanding is infinite. 6 The LORD lifts up the humble; He casts the wicked down to the ground. 7 Sing praises on the harp to our God,

I honestly stopped feeling good about taking my marriage vows. Those feelings came from being violated, I thought when I said I do, my marriage would be the very thing I could trust no matter what. The lies, infidelity, betrayal, and brokenness changed my language and that's when bitterness and anger was coming to the surface since it was rising in me. At that point, I knew it was time to get up and move on from that dead thing called my marriage. I had to stop trying to breathe life into that situation because my breakthrough season was being delayed and it was becoming a hindrance, God wasn't going to bless my mess under any circumstances. As hard as it appeared I had to admit to myself it was time to climb into God's chariot and keep it moving. Yep, that was it, my mind was made up, and guess what, "I'm justified" in doing so.

Psalms Chapter 91 verse 1

1 He who dwells in the secret place of the Most High shall abide under the shadow of the Almighty.

CHAPTER FOUR
"Time To Meditate On Things"

Joshua Chapter 1 Verses 7-8

7 Only be strong and very courageous, that you may observe to do according to all the law which Moses My servant commanded you; do not turn it to the right hand or to the left, that you may prosper wherever you go. 8 This book of the Law shall not, that you may observe to do according to all that is written in it. For then you will make your way prosperous, and then you will have good success. 9 Have I not commanded you? Be strong and of good courage; do not be afraid, nor be dismayed, for the LORD your God is with you wherever you go"

I HAVE SCARS BECAUSE I HAVE A HISTORY. The mental torment, self-inflicted wounds, failed marriage, self-neglect, insecurities, alcoholism, marijuana use, my childhood, and failed relationships kept me in bondage. I had to ask myself constantly, "How long am I willing to let myself be consumed by these things? I asked for God to change my mind, for restoration, for a major shifting, and stretching, but why am I fighting it and why keep looking back?" I also declared that my drought season was over and Satan had no place in my life, but mentally I was still staying stuck.

47

I went into a deep meditation after I came from service on March 19, 2017, no one was home which made it even better, so I could have complete silence.

Meditation was now something I began practicing regularly, it gave me that much-needed opportunity to reflect on things and create a sense of peace. I am an avid writer, not by profession, but writing my thoughts out gives me an outlet and a release. After the meditation process, I write my issues out and think about how I can resolve them and grow from them. The first thing I had to tackle was my childhood and how those issues affected my decision process throughout my wilderness journey.

My childhood was rough and growing up in my early years I survived a lot both mentally and physically. I remember on one incident, being sent to a neighbor's house to get a stick of butter and when I got in there he began to touch my hair and kiss on me at the age of 8. I tried to run but he grabbed my arm and said if I told anyone he would hurt me. I ran and told my mother and my Uncle Sammy confronted the neighbor. I witnessed a man lying on my living room floor with gunshot wounds that he sustained from my stepfather. All we were told was that he tried to break into our house. On another occasion, my mother and stepfather decided to part ways due to his physical abuse, but I had no choice in the matter all I was told was to go pack my things because I was going with him.

A lot of the problems I faced in my early years weren't mine, I inherited them from my parents. Most adult's pain comes from childhood hurt that was never healed. In my earlier years, it was very hard for me to overcome a lot of the mental and physical damage I endured. It took years for me to forgive my parents. I would be lying if I said that it was an easy process because, in all honesty, it wasn't. I was looking and longing for an apology from them that I never believed I was going to get. My way of dealing with them was not being present in their lives at all, I thought maybe if this happened then they would feel like had I felt for years. As I grew older and had my own children I vowed to never let them encounter an ounce of what I did and to show them that through it all I would never leave their side. If issues arise we would conquer them together.

My mother and I would reconcile many times, but when I felt we were headed down the same path of destruction I would back away. No matter how much we were at odds I never once opened my mouth and became disrespectful towards her at all. I stayed away to keep from reliving all the hurt I personally felt from my past childhood experiences. During the last seven years of her life, she had numerous hospitalizations and even though we were not on speaking terms I still rushed to her aid. In fact, her husband made me her liaison over her medical care because he personally felt that after all we have been through, this would give us a bonding experience. I never held my personal feelings against her treatment, I made sure she received the best quality of care possible. My spirit and heart wouldn't allow me to be bitter over things, because as stubborn as I was I knew my very existence was due to her as well as my dad. During my father's final hospitalization, my brother Mike had to make the decision whether to let him live in a vegetated state or release him. We made the best decision there was and that was to release him.

My mother's final hospitalization was what made me realize that I have to take time and meditate on what I really wanted God to do in my life. I received a call from my brother the day I received my certificate for completion of Bible College. He stated that I needed to get down to the hospital as soon as I could it didn't look well for my mother. As I entered the hospital doors I became overwhelmed with tears, because it was as if I knew this time things were much different for her. I made my way to the intensive care unit, only to arrive at my mother's room and she was excited to see me. I told her to rest up and wiped the tears from her eyes kissed her on her cheek and hugged her fragile body so tight. My mother apologized and told me she was so sorry for everything and she loved me. I tried to fight back the tears but couldn't, I responded, "All is well Mommy."

I had to forgive my mother not just for her but for me. I pulled out my certificate and trophy and showed them to her and the smile that came across her face warmed my heart. Her response was I knew you would be great in all you do and I'm so proud of you. I stayed by her side until visiting hours were over, but never left the hospital in fear of her leaving me. Hours later my brothers, stepfather, aunt, uncle, and I had a conference with the doctors because it was putting a strain on my mother's heart for her to breathe on her own and we had to decide to put her on a ventilator for comfort. We all were in agreement and while they were transitioning her we decided to go home, get freshened up, grab something to eat, and return to the hospital. As we were leaving I received a call for us to turn around because her heart rate was rapidly elevating, and her laboratory results showed signs of septic shock. My heart dropped because I knew what this meant, that eventually septic shock would start attacking her organs and it wouldn't be long before she would be leaving us. I explained everything to my siblings and family members.

As we tried to come to grips with everything we were allowed to visit her and sit, the visiting hours were uplifted. We all remained by her side and each one of us had conversations with her while she lay asleep. I noticed that every time my brothers and I would whisper in her ears tears would roll down her face. I had to try to remain strong for my brothers and stepfather. I made the call to all my mother's grandchildren, nieces, and nephews that all needed to be by her side at this time because things had taken a turn for the worse. Then I received word that my cousin, my mother's niece, who was like a sister to me, that all had taken a part in raising her, was admitted to the University Of Maryland Medical Center Intensive Care unit and was fighting for her life as well. I couldn't understand why my family was being attacked like this, I can't fathom anymore. The week before that, my husband came and took everything out of our house, plus the power was turned off. I asked God to let me know what was going on and my faith was at stake because who did I trust him or satan?

As everyone started arriving to accompany us at the hospital, the attending physician told us it was time to have a family conference and decide which way to go with her treatment. We all met with the attending physician and my mother's covering nurse, we were informed that a turnaround process was not likely to take place because her organs had begun to shut down, and if we decided to let the progress take place she would eventually go into cardiac arrest which was likely to result in a painful death. My brother was against it, and my older brother and stepfather were on the same page as me, we didn't want to see her suffer any longer. It began to be a debate between my stepfather's nephew and me so I decided to remove myself from the room and spend the remainder of time with my mother, comforting her. My oldest nephew broke down and said he had to leave because he couldn't take all this confusion, he kissed my mother on her cheek said his final goodbyes and told me to call him.

My brother said that he wanted me to have a one-on-one honest conversation about the whole ordeal. I broke down to him what the doctors were saying and the current process that our mother was going through. He said that he was in disagreement because he didn't understand what was happening. Now that he understood he agreed with us. I told my family that I think we all needed to stay surrounded by my mother until she transitioned and that's what we did remained united. As they removed her breathing tube I grabbed her hand tightly and made a vow that I was not leaving until she was removed from her room and that my mother was going to be handled with dignity. After the removal of the tubing, we were greeted by the ICU team with a blanket to place over her as she made her final transition. Not even an hour after I heard the death rattle coming from her and moments later my brothers and stepfather surrounded her as she took her final breath. I held her hand and laid my head on her chest and experienced her final breath. Something I will never forget. I raised my head with tears in my eyes and in a matter of minutes I noticed her transitioning and fell apart.

I mustered up the strength to speak a final prayer over my mother's lifeless body with my family before they came to remove her remains. The nursing staff let me assist with preparing her body and removing all tubing before placing her in a body bag. I was also able to place her toe tags on, brush her hair, and wipe her down, they even let me go as far as zipping up the body bag and kissing her before they made the transfer to the morgue. My cousins, daughters, aunt, uncle, and brothers stared in awe because they couldn't believe I was able to handle it. Truth be told I wasn't but I wanted to ensure my mother was given the proper send-off. As we gathered her things from the room, I knew that it was time for me to take my position as the matriarch of the family and start preparing for her funeral.

Over the week leading to my mother's funeral I barely got any sleep, to be honest I think I averaged at least two hours of sleep if that. It was not only my mother's death that kept me up but whether I was going to remain in my self-made prison or trust God and take my rightful place in His palace. For me, I lacked faith in so many areas in my life and for those very reasons, I lack trust in anything or anyone. I do know that I had to make a change and it had to happen soon or I would probably end up sentenced to life in a prison that I created for myself. I decided to trust in God with everything in me, it was only right because with all I have sustained over this period, I remained at peace and it was only by His grace and mercies.

In order for me to continuously grow in Christ as I wanted to and set all of myself aside, I had to become desperate for Christ. I couldn't just continue to show up to worship, bible study, and noonday service anymore just in a physical realm. I had to show up in a spiritual realm as well, hungry for God's word. All these things fell apart because God had to completely break me in order to build me up in His image. I couldn't just play it safe anymore, I had to release my pride and allow God to transition me into a new version of me. If God would've kept me the way I was it wouldn't have been long before I would self-destruct by repeating the same cycles again. The only thing that was keeping me in my prison mentality and delaying my blessings from flowing was my wicked thinking and self-doubt. My problem was that I was so afraid of being called out and public humiliation.

To everyone, I presented this image as being well put together, but that was far from the case, I was a total mess on the inside, and despite my appearance that was the truth. I started my meditation sessions again and this time I did things a lot differently. I open up in prayer and then begin reading a Psalm before the meditation. I purchased my women's NKJV devotional bible back on October 10, 2015, but never used it as much as I have over the last year. In the bible, I was glancing through it and what drew me to Psalms was the description under the book, it stated that every human emotion, every ounce of pain, every longing, every sorrow and sadness, and every good and perfect feeling you've ever know is located in this book.

As I began reading and meditating on the chapters in Psalm I began to deal with my darkness, and my anger, and that's when I began to receive balance in my life. It released me from my hurt and past disappointments. Psalm chapter 37 verses 8 through 10 reads, 8 "Cease from anger, and forsake wrath; Do not fret- it only causes harm. 9 for evildoers shall be cut off; But those who wait on the LORD, They shall inherit the earth. 10 For yet a little while and the wicked shall be no more; Indeed, you will look carefully for his palace, But it shall be no more."

It was now time to take inventory of who I allowed in my kingdom and what role they played in my life. I had to put people in their proper position and this didn't sit well with a lot of my friends and family. It was necessary as I began seeking God's counsel to obtain freedom from my self-made prison. If I got the positioning mixed up, people would take that opportunity to throw my thinking off and confuse my life. They would automatically put me back into the prison cell I was trying and fighting so hard to escape from. Genesis 40 The Prisoners' Dreams. In that scripture, The butler is the cup barrier and the baker makes things out of nothing both were servants of the King Pharaoh. That taught me that you must always be aware and very careful about who you allow to hold and make things happen for you.

Not everyone and everything connected to you is of God's lineage. I had to evaluate who was pushing me to tap into my purpose, and who was stopping me from being obedient to God. My peace was now attached to who I trusted. The place God is taking me is too intense for me to carry people who don't believe in His vision. At this critical point in my life, I needed to be surrounded by people who were not speaking against God's spirit, doubting what the Lord was speaking, and people who refused to take me back to that place of hurt. If people walk away from me I have to let them continue to travel on without me. I want to do what God has called me to do and I can't stay stuck in people's insecurities. I declare that I am trusting God and I know where he delivered me from and I'm not going back there. I'm putting all those relationships to death and raising to where God is calling me. I must lay hold onto God's word and His holy spiritfor my freedom and it won't be in vain.

CHAPTER FIVE

"People Won't See You Until You See You"

Psalm Chapter 3- A Psalm of David when he fled from Absalom his son.

1   LORD, how they have increased who trouble me!
    Many are they who rise up against me.

2   Many are they who say of me,
    "There is no help for him in God."

3   But You, O Lord, are a shield for me,
    My glory and the One who lifts up my head

4   I cried to the LORD with my voice,
    And He heard me from His holy hill.
    Selah

5   I lay down and slept;
    I awoke, for the LORD sustained me.

6   I will not be afraid of ten thousand of people
    Who have set themselves against me all around.

7   Arise, O LORD;
    Save me, O my God!
    For you have struck all my enemies on the
    cheekbone;
    You have broken the teeth of the ungodly.

8   Salvation belongs to the LORD.
    Your blessings is upon Your people Selah

I AM A SURVIVOR, I AM A CHILD OF GOD, and

ALL FORMER THINGS HAD TO BE DESTROYED..... This journey for me didn't happen overnight and to be exact it took me over 40 years to escape from the prison I locked myself in before I took the walk of victory. I will admit it wasn't something I did on my own, it was God who came into my life because I wasn't willing to submit to Him, He gracefully broke me.

When you start to see yourself properly you're not going to be willing to submit to your old behaviors or allow people to take you back into the place that God has delivered you from. Many won't understand your growth in what God has developed in you. For me, I've lost a lot during this time of development. For years I was considered the person who consumed with alcohol became very comedic and loved to dance while entertaining everyone, but once I decided to let God use me people's perceptions of me changed. I became, to many, stuck up and holier than thou. She thinks she's better than everyone because she got saved and went to that church and she got a new set of friends.

That's far from the case, those friends are my cousins and because we serve an all-time God, he positioned those family members around me to protect me, strengthen me, and for us to grow in him together, my support system. When you grow your whole circle should grow as well, it's not a single mission, and it's for everyone. When you start seeing yourself with renewed vision, people can't accept the fact that they can't no longer treat you or talk to you in any kind of way anymore. That naïve Jelly is no longer on the surface, the Jelly they will now encounter has grown up, she sees life more abundantly, and accepts life more appropriately. It's not arrogance, it's not self-righteousness, and it's not looking down on people. No, it's me knowing where God has delivered me from, the drunken, reckless mouth, profanity-slinging, and don't give a damn attitude don't reside within me anymore. I've asked God to change me, my mindset, and my heart, to release his holy spirit into me, shift me, and deliver me from any hurt, harm, and danger, so those things had to die. They were the very things that kept me in bondage. I'm at a critical stage in my life where I can't settle anymore into what people's perceptions of me are nor am I willing to submit to anyone for their self-gratification.

I still love you as my family and friends, but if you can't accept the calling on my life then we have to continue down a different path. I've invited you to grow with me in Christ and if you decline that invitation I won't judge you, but I will continue without you and we must detach. God is my lifeline and He's the only one who secures my future. So if you can't see me properly and understand why God raised me from the prison I created for myself then let's just say our goodbyes right now and wish each other the best in all our future endeavors. You see the God that I now serve wholeheartedly is my everything, My primary care physician, my therapist, my light, my Alpha, and my Omega. He has brought me out of a dark place so I refuse to look back or let anyone take me on a journey back there.

I CHOOSE LIFE. The funny thing about this is that once you've been set free, you have no choice but to come to the realization that the cell door was never locked. We just finally choose to walk out of those confined walls. Neither God nor Satan placed us there, we did. We get so caught up in life and trying to live in places that weren't even designed for us. We get so attached to living the way man has imagined for us that we fall short every time trying to live up to those images. We attract the wrong people and the wrong things. Failing to realize that they become burdens, grief, self-esteem issues, and depression. We give man full authority to reign supreme over our lives and when all else fails, then we seek God's counsel. Yes, He will never leave us or forsake us but we have left him and forsaken Him, but yet He still forgives us through it all.

Throughout the previous chapters, you've read parts of my story, and you've even taken a glimpse of my struggles, some will be inspired by my story and others may not be, but I hope that you see that God didn't allow me to be permanently hurt or destroyed through my journey. God simply stepped back and let me go through those things until I was willing to submit to the calling on my life, and it wasn't until then that he broke me, restored my vision, and allowed me to see myself properly. That marriage, those many failed relationships, and those lost friendships weren't created or designed for my life. I had to walk through that wilderness period with God traveling behind me until I was willing to let Him take the lead. Once I gave myself properly to Him then He started my restoration process.

I take nothing for granted and I can honestly say that for me He raised my standards higher than they previously were. No longer am I living and not existing, I'm embracing my newness. I enjoy life a lot differently, alcohol and marijuana are no longer my buffer to create a great time. I value my stretching and increasing in God's kingdom, so if you can't add to that then I will have to say goodbye. Yes, I still have a way to go and this is just the beginning so I have no room for any unnecessary distractions that will hinder me from moving forward. I might love you but I have to pick up my mantle and keep walking. No room for negativity because it doesn't reside here anymore. Clubbing is a thing of my past, I only dance for God and His beloved son Jesus who died on the cross for my transgressions and sins, which granted me an opportunity at life.

This may seem a little unorthodox to many, but my greatest lessons have been from my pen and notepad. I took a challenge of God versus Man, on one side of the paper I listed all the good God has done, and on the other side man. Well, we all know who won. God, of course, His list consisted of several pages, and let's keep it real man's list wasn't even a half of page. With this being said why would I choose man over God? I will not even take up a debate on the matter.

I can guarantee you that God is not a man of failure nor does He have malicious intent. Man's agenda is always questionable, whereas God's is never questionable. Now that I see myself properly, I will not give in to former things. You can't tear me down anymore because I have recovered from that. You can't play the victim and I surrender, no, I recovered from that. You can't just show up in my presence and use my kindness for my weakness any longer, no I recovered from that. I refuse to let people waste my time on this journey, for I have a passion for my calling and I must ignore anything that doesn't bring me peace. I refuse to be wrecked in this season. If I can't take anything positive away from you then we must be set apart.

CHAPTER SIX

"No More Excuses, Your Pain Has A Purpose"

Ephesians Chapter One Verses 11 - 13

11 In Him also we have obtained an inheritance, being predestined according to the purpose of Him who works all things according to the counsel of His will, 12. that we who first trusted in Christ should be to the praise of Glory 13. In Him, you also trusted, after you heard the word of truth, the gospel of your salvation; in whom also, having believed, you were sealed with the Holy Spirit of promise,

For me what I have learned and realized throughout my wilderness journey is that I could've accomplished and advanced so many years ago, but I have mastered the art of masking my issues, ways, and thinking with EXCUSES… That was my delay in receiving my guaranteed inheritance from God. My consistent use of excuses had me downplaying my anointing through Christ. They had me on a constant search mission for things God had already predestined in my view and life. I became so blindsided and my view was so obstructed that I was unable to grab my wealth from my inheritance.

I'm not talking about finances, I'm talking about my royalties from God.

I had to learn a lot of lessons the hard way, one of the hardest lessons was that my freedom, my anointing, and who I was called to be were attached to my excuses. Yes, those excuses kept me in bondage longer than I should have been. We must realize that our excuses don't wake up our anointing. Excuses won't wake up the fire God placed down inside of you. As we make preparations to grow we must understand that unless we change our minds will stay stuck and it will keep us from the promises of God. In this season we have to start doing things much differently than before.

I lost my marriage	EXCUSE
I need time to grieve over that heartbreak as well as time to recover	EXCUSE
I still have scars from my childhood	EXCUSE
I'm still broken from my failures	EXCUSE
My finances are a total mess	EXCUSE
My grown children still need me	EXCUSE
I'm raising my child on my own now	EXCUSE
I have to start over again and I have to work overtime to achieve that	EXCUSE

Those excuses kept me from tapping into my kingdom purpose for years and left me stranded in prison when I had a palace awaiting my arrival, the place where God had already prepared for me. My wilderness walk shouldn't have taken me forty plus years to reach the destination where God was ordaining my life to be. Why should I keep making excuses when I have a partnership with God, who is the owner of my salvation? The time is now for me to wake up and be the radical person God has created me to be.

Excuses break miracles and will delay your blessings. It's time to leave the excuses behind and claim everything God has promised you. Your excuses will keep you stagnant in a season where God has planned on blessing and delivering you. Unless you step up and change your mindset and leave the excuses behind you will never be able to elevate to the next level and dimension where God wants to elevate you to. God can't multiply what you have in your hands with excuses. It's time to free yourself dissect that pain, hurt, and disappointment and reach out to grab a hold of where God is calling you. We must be humble and remain in the same spirit where we found God, no I'm not saying stay still, I'm saying continue to worship and praise God for He brought you out of some of the craziest places and didn't embarrass you, nor did He let one single person know what He delivered you from. Your excuses will have you lying flat on your back with layers and layers of dirt and residual piled on top of you when God is trying to breathe life into your situation and raise you up from the dead. You have to determine how bad and how desperate you want God. Now is the time to move out of your comfort zone, come off the sidelines and meet God where He has met you, do your part to claim your inheritance. The time is now to deliver on those promises that you made to God when you asked Him if He delivered you from your situations and set you free.

Time to claim your POWER. Time to claim victory over your pride. The Time is now to claim your mind, your heart, and your life back. The time is now to serve the enemy notice. It's time to reach out on faith and grab hold of your partnership with God. Do you know your faith has value and sustenance to it? Don't let another day go by with your faith being held in captivity by your excuses. Your faith has currency and carries weight, while excuses will leave you powerless and empty. It's time to invite God into your circumstances and let His holy spirit saturate you. Work your faith and not your excuses. Your faith unleashes God's power and invites miracles, signs and wonders. You will never know nor will you ever understand the power of God until you're willing to let go of those excuses and trust in Him wholeheartedly, not on a part-time basis.

Now is the time to demand a difference from your circumstances. Demand different from your disappointments. It's time to forgive all those people who left you defeated. Forgiveness is the beginning of your healing process. You must determine if you want something different or if you want to stay in the same life. Why keep consistently repeating the same cycles year after year? Do you want God or do you want the valueless, powerless, empty promises of man? Do you want the salvation of God or the plantation thinking of man? You have to choose, there can't be any more fence climbing or backbiting. God has created us in such a unique way that once you have decided to trust in Him you will not be able to walk into a room and people see you and your situations the same way ever again. Use your wisdom in your judgments, not your sorry excuses.

So what you've been hurt before, God has created a plan for that. So what your husband or wife left and took everything, God has created a plan for that. So what you were left heartbroken and confused, God has already created a plan for that. So what shame was placed on your name, God has already created a plan for that. So what you have to start from the bottom again, God has a plan for that as well. You must realize in your prison state that the promises and plans of God are so real and have been proven throughout time to be valid, not void. As stated in Jeremiah chapter 29 verses 11 through 14. "For I know the thoughts that I think toward you, says the LORD, thoughts of peace and not of evil, to give you a future and a hope. Then you will call upon Me and go and pray to Me, and I will listen to you. And you will seek Me and find Me when you search for Me with all your heart. I will be found by you, says the LORD, and I will bring you back from your captivity; I will gather you from all the nations and from all the places where I have driven you, says the LORD, and I will bring you to the place from which I cause you to be carried away captive."

What is your plan? Be patient, trust God, and let Him transform you or remain in the wilderness and self-made prison that you have created, having the master copy of keys refusing to change and consistently wrestling in your mind with excuses. It took me forty-plus years, how long are you willing to wait to claim your purpose? You have to choose. I'm here to tell you that you're more valuable than silver, gold, emptiness, defeat, excuses, false promises, and man-made possessions. I know where God delivered, saved, and wrapped his loving arms around me. It was at that very moment that I knew without a shadow of a doubt I wasn't giving negativity, defeat, and reckless behaviors another chance to dominate my life. As long as I had breath in my body and blood streaming freely in my veins, I was going to continuously worship and praise God with full Thanksgiving in my heart. What's keeping and holding you back from obtaining your inheritance?

You must know without a shadow of a doubt that the promises and words of God never lose their power, they hold your riches. He has opened doors for you that no man possibly can. He has saved us and closed doors that no man that resides on this earth can. He has truly made a way out of no way when our backs were against the wall. He keeps your mind at peace when you should've utterly lost your mind. He promoted and elevated us to places we couldn't have on our own. God will deliver you from your poverty mindset when you claim your freedom. God's promises and words have essence and fragrance to them. You will only tap into that fragrance and essence once you come to the end of you and your excuses…

SELF EXAMINATION TIME

For this examination, I'm asking that you use a paper, pen, pencil, or sticky note. For each question write your answer on paper so you can review daily as a reminder to keep you moving forward on your journey from the prison to victory. This examination helped me during some of my darkest times and helped me get freed from my self-made depression. I often reflect on these questions when I doubt my life and God. There are no right or wrong answers because we know where our prison and wilderness journey began.

1. What excuses are holding you back from serving God wholeheartedly?
2. Do I really believe in the love and power of God?
3. What pain, emotions, and memories are you holding onto that need to be healed?
4. What personal relationships do you need to be healed?
5. What is your definition of forgiveness?
6. When you are looking in the mirror, what is your perception of the image reflecting back at you? How do you view yourself? Are you seeing a strong person or a weak-minded person?
7. Is the life you're living Christ-like?
8. What triggers you to lose control in situations?

CHAPTER SEVEN
"Renovation Is Necessary, Time To Get The Mind And Heart In Sync"

Philippians Chapter 2 Verse 5

"Let this mind be in you which was also in Christ Jesus"

Philemon 20

"Yes, brother, let me have joy from you in the Lord; refresh my heart in the Lord."

I would honestly be lying to you if I told you that I didn't know or have an inkling of a clue what I was facing walking down the aisle to accept my husband's hand in marriage. We often see the warning signs but because we refuse to use our wisdom in our thinking, the mind gets clouded by the emotions of our heart. I honestly did think that I was in love and if I got that ring, things would change for the better. As I look back throughout my 11-year marriage, it was lust that kept me there stuck in a place that I knew wasn't where my heart truly was. I know that even though I took that vow before my family, my marriage wasn't ordained by God, but by man. So you won't get confused, as I stated before God doesn't bless any mess. We had so many unresolved issues when we walked down the aisle and I think I was more overwhelmed with the idea of getting married than facing a lot of our underlying issues. That's where everything went wrong.

Often as Christians, we associate anything pertaining to a battle, issue, or problems with satan. Not realizing that a lot of the battles, issues, and problems we encounter begin with our minds versus our hearts. Our minds were designed by God for our daily mental functioning and our thought process. On the other hand, our hearts were designed for our daily functioning as well, but they have other unique attributes such as dealing with our emotions, feelings, and desires those things we crave. 99% of the problems we face begin with the mind and heart not being in sync with one another. Let me go a little deeper from a biblical standpoint. Both the heart and mind were crafted by God to work on one accord to establish a connection and lifeline to Him for peace and understanding. As stated in Proverbs chapter 3 verses 5 and 6, "Trust in the Lord with all your heart, and lean not on your own understanding, in all your ways acknowledge him, and he shall direct your path. *In Romans chapter 12 verse 2 states, "Do not be conformed to this world but be transformed by the renewing of your mind that you may prove what is that's good and acceptable and perfect will of God."*

The battles we face such as depression, low self-esteem, suicidal thoughts, and lack of trust and faith happen because we have the need to want to be in total control over everything but always declare we are Christ-like. Not understanding that the Battles we're currently facing in our minds and hearts, God has already given us grace and freedom. Our constant need to want to have control over any and everything has us living in the bondage of our thinking while wrestling with a man who gave up a living sacrifice, his son Jesus so we can have life more abundantly. A man who climbed up a mountain and then demolished it to rescue us in our time of distress. A man who didn't give up on us when we gave up on ourselves even when we've betrayed Him with our thoughts time and time again. I say wrestling with anything about God, one second is way too long.

We keep wrestling with depression, defeat, our desires, and emotions for way too long delaying our blessings and overflow in a blessed season. Over the course of writing this book, the process has not been easy. I thought in the beginning that by me rehashing the past it would become therapeutic, but that was far from it. Rehashing the past took me back down memory lane and right back to the tomb. I've completed 6 chapters and got jolted. Not by God, but by allowing myself to go back to those places I had once sought refuge from. It's safe to say as mature as I thought I could be in this process, I really wasn't that mature at all to handle everything that came with full exposure. Many times as humans we take on projects to say we accomplished this or that, not doing actual research on the tasks ahead. That's where we have our setbacks at acting way too soon. I knew without a shadow of a doubt that God had placed it in me to release this book so it could be a deliverance to so many people and for winning souls for Christ. So as much as I was on the verge of quitting and walking away I had to continuously push forward and write my book for what He has called me to do save souls just as He saved mine.

Recently I was at work, my profession is a nationally certified clinical hemodialysis technician. I was setting my machines up for the workday and started to analyze the connection and preparation process. Everything needed for treatment must be attached to the dialyzer, at that moment I stopped because I was experiencing conviction. Once my patients arrived for their scheduled treatment and I hooked them up to the dialysis machine I became mesmerized as the blood started flowing from the patient through the exit site, traveling to the dialyzer for purification, removing all the toxins from the blood because the kidneys no longer have the ability to properly function. Once the blood began exiting the dialyzer to the entrance site I began crying at that moment because I realized that if we were to take the dialyzer out of the equation the patient's treatment would not be effective. There will be no purpose for the machine, lines, or patient if the main source of purification is stripped away from it. Then I began to realize that the dialyzer is a representation of God, and if He stripped Himself from us completely how would we be able to survive and how would our daily existence be effective without Him? He is our purification system, and he's the only one that can deliver us from our transgressions and sins. God is the only one who can remove all the toxins from our blood system. I realized that the blood of God still runs deep, still has power, and is still alive. He didn't make any mistakes in creating us, we're wonderfully and uniquely made for a reason and purpose. We just have to get our minds and hearts in sync to work on one accord to tap into our kingdom's purpose. We must stop traveling back, letting people take us back, and delete the tomb from our thought process. We must remove anything or anyone that does not bring peace into our lives and then ask God to restore in us a clean heart and mind.

So I say this to you it's war time, it's time to put on the full armor of God and go stand in position preparing for battle. The time is now to get our hearts and minds in sync with one another and rebuke that spirit of depression, rebuke that spirit of low self-esteem, rebuke that spirit of laziness, rebuke that spirit of self-righteousness, rebuke that control spirit, rebuke that spirit of lust and activate God's Holy Spirit in our lives. We must stop declaring defeat over battles when the only function that God requires from us is to live life accordingly, abundantly, and serve His will. Let not your will be done but God's. God is currently fighting battles on our behalf, you must know you're not alone in this war. God's Holy Spirit is currently in the midst and ready to stand in the forefront to help us gain our victory.

Don't quit or don't give up too soon, because God wants to place that winning spirit back in us, but in order to accomplish that we have to release the controls of our minds and hearts back to Him. Seek His presence in your situations, His presence is His face. The time is now to declare victory and restoration over our lives and stop waiting for someone to minister to our souls and complete that task on our own. As stated in Exodus Chapter 34 verses 1-9 "The Lord, The Lord God, merciful and gracious, long-suffering and abounding in goodness and truth keeping mercy for thousands, forgiving iniquity and transgressions and sin…. In this chapter of Exodus God requested that Moses go up on Mount Sinai alone with two tablets and that no man come with him. Once on the mountain of Sinai God descended in the clouds and stood with Him. A lot of time we think everyone needs to be present and aware of the battles we face in order to win and overcome them. We always require an audience. The battles we're trying to face don't require an audience at all. Just like God requested Moses to come alone and meet Him face to face, bow your head, lift your hands, or even kneel down and begin to worship. This is an example of how God will meet us when He requests us to show up and spark that fire in us. We just have to be willing to cast all our battles upon Him. We won't return the same way we left. He will enlighten your understanding through His presence, which is His face. He has designed us in such a unique way that He knows the thoughts and plans for us, to give us a future and hope as stated in Jeremiah 29 verse 11. We can't declare a win over our battles if we are being consistently impatient. We must exercise patience at all costs because the only one who knows how to tear down and demolish walls is God. He's the beginning and end of all things, our Alpha and Omega. He knows what's standing in our way. God doesn't get us out of situations, He directs our paths on where to go next. He gives us conviction because conviction makes and brings about change. There's a value in waiting on God, it's called FREEDOM. I know without a shadow of a doubt that I'd rather be covered in the full armor of God going into any battle than show up naked. Micah chapter 4 verse 5 states "For all people walk each in the name of his god, but we will walk in the name of the LORD our God forever and ever." It's release time sisters, time to declare the end to our battle with the mind and heart, so we can walk properly clothed into our winning season the place where God has ordained our lives to be.

CHAPTER EIGHT
"I Am Evidence"
(The Letter of Conviction)

Whenever you find yourself in a low dark place after you have overcome so many obstacles, STOP immediately what you're doing at that time and begin crying out to our LORD and SAVIOR for guidance and understanding. Often times when we personally feel we have arrived at a place where we consider ourselves free and delivered, we think our work is complete. In fact, let me step out on a limb and say we began to walk and talk differently, we felt a sense of arrogance start to arise within us. Not realizing that there's a price we have to pay for that freedom and that our walk must stay consistent due to the sacrifice that's attached to it. Yes, we've made it out of the prison stages of our lives, but what we must realize is our freedom comes with natural consequences. Natural consequences are outcomes that happen as a result of behaviors that are not planned. The end of my prison journey was not easy for me because I had to do a self-evaluation and reflect on my behaviors and once that process was completed then I was allowed to begin making preparations for my release. What you must understand is that accountability must take place for all your previous actions and behaviors before you're able to crossover.

76

Let's use for example the children of Israel, their journey in the wilderness was only supposed to be a 40-day process but ended up being 40 years due to their disobedience and unbelief. They got cursed with 40 years because they failed to take possession of the land God promised, the land of milk and Honey. EXODUS chapter 3 verse 8 And I have come down to deliver them out of the hand of the Egyptians and bring them out of that land to a good and broad land, a land flowing with milk and honey, to the place of the Canaanites, the Hittites, the Amorites, the Perizzites, the Jebusites.) It's our chronic disbelief in God and standing in our own understanding that has sentenced us to longer prison terms than we deserve. For 40-plus years I stayed confined to a prison cell as stated in a previous chapter because of my unwillingness to submit, my selfishness, and my unbelief. What I had no knowledge of was that for me to begin the process of transitioning into walking in newness, I had to realize that the words of God stand true and the promises will never come back void. The many reasons why it took me so long to inherit anything from God was because I refused to honor, submit, and serve. So yes His promises were before my reach, but God wasn't willing to let me mishandle them like I did my own life. As I accepted God as my Lord and Savior, trusted in who was sent forth to be my covering, Pastor Tony Smith, and became a faithful water walker, then things began to fall off of me. Those things had to die, my nasty attitude, self-entitlement spirit, depression, chronic negative thinking, and stubbornness had to be purged out of my body. Once that transition took place, I was finally released to partake in "The Promise."

When you arrive don't let your happiness blind you to the point that you think you don't still have work to do, I would be remised if I wasn't honest with you. In NUMBERS 14:11 it says, "And the LORD said to Moses, "How long will this people despise me? Despite all the signs that I have done among them?" So my questions to you are, "How long are you willing to remain in your wilderness walk and not trust God after He gave you all the signs that His mercy and grace endure forever? How long are you willing to remain in a place that was designed to build you, but because of your thinking and unwillingness to submit has torn you down without guidance? How long will it take you to realize that the promises of God are Yes and Amen?

I pray that this book has given you some powerful tools and that my willingness to be open enough to share my life gives you hope and understanding that our journeys were ordained in our Mother's womb. Our journeys don't end until we cross over from this earthly realm. In my lifetime I've encountered and endured so much, but through those times I have learned many lessons. I learned that my pain truly has a purpose. But today I'm pleased to inform you that I'm finally embarking on my Victory Season. Once I learned to become submissive and obedient CANCER had to bow down. As of March 21, 2018, I'm cancer free. That's not of my own doing, but God's grace and mercy found it fit to deliver me from what was designed to destroy me physically. I had to learn how to trust God's timing and obtain the lessons in whatever season I was currently in no matter how impossible my circumstances appeared. Towards the end of my failing marriage, I should've been left in complete disarray, BUT GOD… He found it fit for me to come out not looking like what I've been through, I can honestly say that I never once succumbed to that situation. I can't remember one day that I had a pity party, cried, or tried to defend my name. By me believing in God wholeheartedly I prayed on it numerous times and released it to a higher power to handle. I couldn't fight that battle on my own, it had to be released so I could move forward with my victory walk. As stated in Hebrews 11:6 "And without faith it is impossible to please him, for whoever would draw near to God must believe that he exists and he rewards those who seek Him." In your Victory walk don't think mistakes and mishaps will not take place, they will you just have to do an evaluation of it and get up from them and dust yourself off and press forward towards the calling of your life.

THE LETTER OF CONVICTION

Dear Jelly,

You must know without a shadow of a doubt that the God we serve is so amazing and His love is unconditional, everlasting, and his mercies endure forever. Your birth was ordained for God's glory, and fulfillment of His living will, and wasn't a mistake or punishment. Your trials, tribulations, and tests were created for this moment right here, in your book, to share your testimony to save souls for Christ. Please understand that the 43 years you spent wandering lost around the wilderness were necessary to guide you to your victory walk. You couldn't decipher how to live and remain in victory being unstable, disobedient, stuck, ungrateful, stubborn, and unwilling to be taught. If God didn't break you when He did, you would still be lost in the valley when He ordained you to dwell on the mountaintop.

Those tests you endured were designed to build your faith in God, remove you out of the equation, and teach you to stand behind the cross, instead of you always trying to walk in front of it. God had to make you understand that everything in this world must be approved and ordained through Him, that people of this world won't complete you, and his Purpose is the only thing that will complete you. If God's purpose were easy, it would never be properly fulfilled by any of His children. Jelly, I need you to take some time and think about these things. If God had used you over the course of those43 years, would you be able to handle the blessings? Would you be able to keep your grip on the mantle? Howcould you break those generational curses that plagued your entire family? Depression, Attention Deficit Disorder, Low self-esteem, Unforgiving heart, Lack of Unity, Abandonment issues, and poverty-strickenmindsets. Our God is of order and He's not going to justhand you things without preparation. If that was the casehe would only give his Purpose the minimal. God loves tosee things he placed in his children's hands fulfilled in amaximum capacity. Your unwillingness to be submissivemade you disqualified to partner with God and lay handson His promise.

There were so many times you cried in silence to God, He wasn't ignoring your cries, He was trying to get you to hold your head up and follow Him. That delay wasn't of satan, your delay was of God. He couldn't bless you with your immature mindset, unstable heart, and unbalanced way of moving. I must admit, from living through you, that you were unteachable, unwilling to be submissive, and hold your head up when told to. Those few acts alone were prime examples that showed Him you weren't prepared to receive a blessing at all. Your body was specifically created as a sacred temple and you never

81

valued it as He did. If I can be honest with you, your value depreciated by letting others mishandle and befoul it. You never understood that you're part of a Royal Priesthood, He couldn't pour into a damaged temple that He fearfully and wonderfully made.

Those prophecies that were given to you were instructions for you not to touch them, you placed your hands on them anyway. Once again our Purpose was delayed. How can God trust you with His valuable Purpose when you can't even properly carry His mantle? Especially when the mantle carries less weight than His purpose.

You keep running to the altar and begging for forgiveness and to be used. So is that for your glory or his? Now is the time for you to surrender it all because your children and your children's children are depending on you to walk a different path than you witnessed. It's time for you to go to Jericho to be retaught, stripped naked, submit, be fully broken, and let things that fell off of you lay without you being resistant. I must let you know that the process is not going to be an easy one, accepting discipline from God is necessary to complete the process. Do you know that the access we have to God grants us the power to redeem the benefits of Jesus' blood? You must realize that everything God gives us grants us access to greater, we just look at the cup half empty when the cup is filled to capacity. Once this process in Jericho is completed then you will regain your strength and power to walk in purpose. Now I'm not saying once you start walking in purpose your mission is accomplished, because it's not. You will be able to deal with opposition without doubt and hesitation. Every level that you encounter thereafter you must shift the atmosphere, but not submit to it without consulting with God first.

At the place you are, I find it totally necessary to be really up close and in your face, because that's the only pattern I've seen from you over the years that seems to capture you're attention. Mild discipline doesn't stimulate you at all, hardcore punishment is what seems to break you and that's when you're willing to submit. You're not the individual who determines how the battle will end, God is. So I need you to stop running from the things that have been ordained to push you into purpose because my lifeline is connected to it as well. I can't be freed if you keep consulting yourself without considering me, we complete each other. If we're not unified how can we move forward? So my immature companion it's time for you to unplug from social media, your own personal desires, and anything you're hiding that's not ordained by God and maintain your focus. I can't enter into our Holy place because of your procrastinating spirit. You have to use the time designed for you to unplug and complete those tasks left undone. Not weeks from now but upon receipt of this letter. We're at year 50 and we have no time to dwell in the places of this world when we are designed for Kingdom. This was a very draining process writing this letter, but that's the way I can seem to speak to you. You must know that I love you and see so much greatness in you that you fail to see in yourself and I don't see me winning without your partnership in this journey.

Love Angellic

Made in the USA
Columbia, SC
14 September 2024

42171100R00053